ACE THE
GRE
Writing Assessment

TIM AVANTS

SOURCEBOOKS, INC.
NAPERVILLE, ILLINOIS

Published by Sourcebooks, Inc.
P.O. Box 4410, Naperville, Illinois 60567-4410
(630) 961-3900
Fax: (630) 961-2168
www.sourcebooks.com

Printed and bound in the United States of America.
BG 10 9 8 7 6 5 4 3 2 1

To my lovely wife Berna

Contents

CHAPTER ONE

Introduction to the Writing Assessment

The following is designed to provide general information needed to make your Writing Assessment Test pain free. The information includes procedures for testing, assessment content, and various items that will prove useful throughout the entire testing process.

1. The Two GRE Writing Assessment components
2. The Official 250 Questions downloadable at the ETS website
3. Procedures
4. Using the GRE Word Processor
5. The Scoring System for the GRE Essays
6. Score Reports

The ETS has an official website where you can download 250 official questions free: 125 for the Issue segment and 125 for the Argument segment. The student receives a question at random during the test. The site is located at www.gre.org/writing.html.

Like most computer adaptive tests, the writing assessment section will have a tutorial prior to the beginning of the writing assessment. This will allow you time to acquaint yourself with the computer. Pencil and paper will be provided should you need to make notes while you are writing. Once you have completed the Issue section, you can move on to the Argument section. However, once you exit the Issue segment, you cannot return, even if you finished with time remaining. In addition, there is no break between the Issue and the Argument sections.

The testing system does not allow you to return to either of the two essays once you've moved on. There is no spell check, so be sure you check over your work.

Two different readers score each section of the Assessment for a total of four readers. All of the scores are averaged to make one score for the Argument and Issue sections together. Let's look at a sample score.

Issue	**Argument**
Reader 1=3	Reader 3=5
Reader 2=3	Reader 4=4
Total=6	Total=9

The total of the Issue and the Argument sections equals 15. Divide 15 by 4 (number of readers) and that equals 3.75. The average would be rounded up to a score of 4 on the Writing Assessment, because any score over 50% is rounded up. Here, the 3.75 is over the 3.5, so we rounded the score up to 4.

You will also receive a percentile rank. For instance, a rank of 70% indicates that you scored higher than 70% of the test-takers and 30% of test-takers scored higher than you.

Scores are mailed to you and to the schools in about three weeks. Percentile rank is not reported to the schools.

The schools determine how much weight that they want to give to the scores of the Writing Assessment when considering applicants to graduate school. You should check with the school you want to attend prior to taking the exam. Be advised, though, that many schools will look at a high score on the Writing

Assessment and allow that to offset a lower score on the Quantitative section, especially if the student is applying to a graduate program in the humanities, such as English or Sociology.

Before we begin on particular test items, we need to review some fundamentals of sentence structure and punctuation to ensure success. Most often, I read (as a college professor) excellent essays that only receive a C because of punctuation mistakes that cause problems with logic. These are most often problems that could easily be avoided with an hour of review.

CHAPTER TWO:

Punctuation

The Comma

The comma is used to set off words, several-word phrases, or clauses. There are two basic rules I like to use when determining when to put a comma in a sentence.

A. The Formal Rule

If you have an independent clause, and something comes to the left of the subject, and it's not an article, and it's not an adjective, set it off with a comma.

> **Example:** <u>On the way</u>, [we stopped at the store.]
>
> S—-V
>
> Independent Clause (IC)

The big boy ate the candy.

Art. -adj.-S—-V-art. -Direct Object (DO)

There is no comma in the second example, because it does not follow the rule (the words before the subject are an article[art.] and an adjective[adj.]). We said that the clause must be an independent clause.

That means it must be able to stand by itself. If it does not, it's not an independent clause. If it's not independent, it's either a sentence fragment or a dependent clause. A dependent clause will usually have a word at the very beginning of it that will make it depend on another sentence to come after it to complete the thought. For example:

When I was a boy, I ate candy

Dep. Clause (DC)—IC

The dependent clause usually has a subject and a verb, and it is referred to as a subordinate clause. The subordinator makes an independent clause dependent. Generally, a subordinator is usually a preposition: in, on, after, under, whenever, before, while, among, next, toward.

Not all dependent clauses necessarily have a subject and verb, but, for the sake of discussion, we will talk in generalizations. Therefore, although a clause or phrase which comes before an independent clause may not have both a subject and verb, we usually set it off by using both rules described here.

Along the banks, fires were glowing.

Around the bend, a truck had crashed.

In December, we stay in the house. After dinner, we ate dessert.

Up the coast, there were many sea gulls.

Under the table, the boy played carelessly.

B. The Gut Rule

Simply put, if there is no trauma, do not add a comma.

I don't want to oversimplify, but we can usually look at the sentence and determine what is pertinent information and what is extra. By doing this, combined with the formal rule, we can figure out where to put the comma. For example:

Today, I went to the store.
Yesterday, I went shopping.

The important information comes after the comma in both sentences. It is not really important that the person went to the store today. Simply the fact that he went to the store is important. The same logic is true with the second sentence. Now, if I want to make the information of today just as important as the fact that I went to the store, I will integrate that into the structure of the independent clause. For example:

I went to the store today.
I went shopping yesterday.
I want to eat chicken tonight.

Let's view these sentences in how they are actually spoken. If the time tag is at the beginning of the sentence, there will be a slight pause in the sentence before I start to say the information in the independent clause. This pause is a change in tone that leads me to believe that I must include a comma. Note that the tone goes down where the comma is inserted, and it rises again after the comma in the independent clause.

Tone: _____

Today, I went shopping.

I went shopping today.

Tone: _____

Tone and stress are two different things. I can stress a certain word, but that does not necessarily mean that I automatically put in a comma. Likewise, I now feel compelled to dispel a myth. Most of us, and wrongly I might add, were taught to put a comma in a sentence if we pause. Well, that's not always true. Following that logic, let's look at an example. Let's assume that my wife saw me at the store with a beautiful woman, and she asked me about it after I made it home. Following the logic of the rule we are usually taught in Elementary school, we would punctuate my reply with the commas indicated. Keep in mind that I will choose my answer very carefully to her question, because I will definitely live with my answer for the rest of my life.

QUESTION:
Who was that woman you were with at the store?

ANSWER:
S,s,s,ss,hh,he,ee ii,i,is,s,s,ss mm,mm,yy
ff,f,ffr,rr,iiennd. (She is my friend.)

I hope you get my point. So, let's forget about the rule that we must always put in a comma if there is a pause in a sentence. Let's follow the rule below:

If there is no trauma, don't add a comma.

We almost always need commas after transitional phrases, which we've discussed before, because they come before an independent clause (IC).

Afterthought

An afterthought needs to come after an IC. It signals extra information, but at the end of a sentence. There may be contention with a professor about the use of commas in this regard, because only you can determine if the afterthought is actually extra information or if it is, in fact, pertinent.

We sat down and ate candy, and old bread.

I saw the man with one arm, and also his dog

I ate the whole chicken, and then had dessert.

We played football, and basketball.

However, a sentence with one subject and two predicates (verbs) or two objects does not need a comma.

He ran and walked. He ate bread and cheese.

Appositive

An appositive commonly renames a noun, and commas usually set it off. The noun and the other phrase renaming or describing it have reference in common, one normally renaming another. Some appositives are not set off, and these are called restricted, because their address is only directed (restricted) to the noun or its equivalent next to it. Again, restricted means that one does NOT add any commas, because the description is restricted or limited to the word or phrase directly next to it.

Those set off with commas are <u>nonrestricted.</u>

The fat boy, <u>the one with the glasses</u>, sat on my ice cream.

I like sports, <u>namely boxing</u>, more than studying.

Her most outstanding characteristic, <u>being nice</u>, brought her luck.

One thing, <u>running</u>, is better than most anything I know.

The man, <u>Jon</u>, lit a smoke.

The General, <u>Rommel</u>, won the battle.

He bought her a gift for her birthday, <u>a cruise</u>.

The underlined words are the appositives. All the underlined phrases rename or describe the noun before it, except in the last sentence, where cruise renames gift. Here, a cruise is an afterthought, so we offset it with a comma.

Interjections

We said before that interjections interrupt. I also said that they are utterly useless, and that is generally true, at least in the context in which we saw them. But, an interjectory phrase can be highly useful information, but it is, nevertheless, extra. It can be a transition that points direction of an argument, or it may comment somehow. For example:

1. I think, however, life is good.
2. She said, convincingly enough, that she was innocent.
3. I, oddly enough, feel tired.
4. He looked like, but I'm not sure, the man who shot the dog.

EXPLANATIONS:

1. Here, however signals a change in the direction of a conversation.
2. Convincingly enough comments on the subject matter of the sentence.
3. Oddly enough comments on the content of the message.
4. The clause but I'm not sure interrupts to give extra information and comment on the content of the sentence.

>
> **NOTE:**
>
> *Because we have broken the structure of the sentence, interrupted it, we must set apart the interjections (phrases and clauses) with commas.*

Independent Clauses

When we join two independent clauses with a comma, we must have a coordinating conjunction connecting them. These words are coordinating conjunctions when connecting two independent clauses; when moved in the superstructure, they may take on different functions. Hence, the coordinating conjunctions are situated between the two Independent clauses (ICs)

BOYFANS: But, Because, or, yet, for, and, nor, neither, so

I went, but I didn't enjoy myself.

I want money, because I'm hungry.

I will go to Egypt, or I'll return home.

I ate, yet I'm still hungry.

For

Do not use this. It is somewhat archaic. He stayed behind, for he was ill. For generally has the sense of a causal relationship, but the indication of the relationship between the event in the first clause and that in the second is more ambiguous than with the usage of because. Plus, it is chiefly British English (Br.E.).

I walked a mile, and I lifted weights.

I won't run, nor will I walk.

I don't drink alcohol, neither does he.

[Notice the inverted word order in the second clauses with nor and neither.]

I drank coffee, so did he.

I wanted ice, so I went to the store.

Series of Things

When listing a series of things, commas are used between sentence fragments, single-word phrases, and descriptive phrases.

Sentence Fragments

I went home, ate some food, walked the dog, and went to bed.

I stayed up late, got up early, and worked out.

My son kicked the ball, cleaned the garage, and set up the basketball hoop.

I said that the verb phrases were sentence fragments, because they all lack a subject. Therefore, they can be linked by use of a comma. But, if they had subjects, we would need to add a coordinating conjunction (c/c). They can be linked a different way, which we will discuss later. Always look for the subject and verb when punctuating a sentence, and you can determine how to set it up.

Single-Word Phrases

He sings, dances, and plays.

He bought an apple, a toy, paper, and a pen.

I saw Bob, Mary, and Ted.

NOTE:

If there are three or more items, we need to put an article before the last item in the series. If there are only two items, we do not need a comma at all.

Descriptive Phrases

The big, fat, ugly bear ate the meat.

The old, rusty, worn-out plane crashed.

The oldest, prettiest, and most majestic tree was cut down.

NOTE:

We put the commas between the adjectival phrases, because they all modify the same noun, so, if the adjectival is not describing the word in front of it, we must insert commas between them, unless, as in the last sentence, an adverb describes an adjective. Likewise, with the sentence fragments, or the verb phrases, one subject is involved in several actions, so a comma must set off each particular unit.

Semicolons

Semicolons link independent clauses. Plus, they link sentence fragments in block language.

Independent Clauses

Linking two independent clauses with a semicolon suggests some sort of a causal relationship. The first clause acts as a cause, whereas the second clause is the effect.

I ate; I got sick.

She has her life; I have mine.

They went their way; we went ours

The old man died first; his wife died within a month.

The superstructure (both clauses linked together to make one complete sentence) itself could be diagrammed like this:

General Statement; Specific Statement

If we wanted to change the pattern of the sentences, we could rewrite them:

Because I ate, I got sick.

Since she has her life, I have mine.

Because they went their way, we went ours.

Because the old man died, his wife died.

This does not mean that all sentences fit into this category, but it's a good attack to use when working with the semicolon in superstructures that contain only two clauses. This involves writing style and the ability to change your sentence structure.

Semicolon with a Series of Independent Clauses

Again, this is more common in technical structures, but academic writing requires the use of it, especially in term papers. In term papers, it's often necessary to work with series in quotes, especially if you include the support of many scholars, or, perhaps even more common, if you refute specific contentions a scholar has concerning your topic. The series may be introduced with a colon.

> Professor X contends Lord Tennyson's writing had a three-fold function: Primarily, it acted as a cathartic function after the sudden demise of his best friend; Secondly, the repetition of his work vicariously honed his skills throughout the next thirty years, in spite of the silence; Lastly, his writings acted as, and continue to do so, a bridge for contemporary scholars to glimpse into the mind of one of the most prolific writers the West has ever known.

Using the semicolon in this arrangement allows the writer to organize his work and that of others in a concise pattern. Conciseness is a valuable asset in an effective paper. We want to use semicolons to link two independent clauses to set a very serious tone. Including a coordinating conjunction sets a more light and airy tone. Sometimes, that's not appropriate to convey your message.

Reminder: Your audience determines the diction you use; the diction sets the tone. Of course, your diction or word choice must be exemplary of an educated person, one who is insightful and well spoken.

Colon

Use the colon to a) introduce a list or series of items and b) to express extremely important information. The colon must follow an independent clause.

I did three things: ate, exercised, and studied.

I have had problems with the following functions: working with graphs, setting the tabs, and copying the text.

He wrestled with three scenarios: It was necessary to find the brain tumor in time; The donor was dying; The consent form was lost.

He wrestled with three scenarios: It was necessary to find the brain tumor in time, but the donor was dying, and the consent form was lost.

Tip: Only capitalize the beginning of the information after the colon if it includes an independent clause or if it is only one word. Also, each IC is capitalized in the series with the semicolon, because the semicolon acts like a period, signifying a terminal break in the continuity of that IC, whereas, if we join the IC(s) with a C/C, the new IC is not capitalized. In the last example, this sentence carries a less serious tone, less gravity than that of the superstructure before wherein the IC(s) are joined by semicolons. Furthermore, in formal writing, one needs to vary the sentence patterns; therefore, the use of semicolons should be used more frequently when dealing with structures like these. In the next structure, we need to follow our technical rule and our gut rule closely to determine where to put the commas. Think in terms of formality.

S——VC/C-S——-V/Sub. S——V

After the game, <u>we went to the store</u>, but we came home when it began to rain.

EXPLANATION:

If you have an IC, and something is to the left of the subject, and it's not an article, and it's not an adjective, set it off by a comma. Here, the word game fits that description. So, we put a comma after the word game, because game is a noun. We put a comma before but, because but is a coordinating conjunction, which links two independent clauses. Looking at the dependent clause, when fits the description at the beginning of our explanation. However, when is a subordinator, so a comma does not set it off. A time word, usually one which indicates a duration of time, or a preposition before the subject tell us that we're dealing with a dependent clause, which must be set off from the IC if it precedes the IC in the superstructure. Let's invert the structure of the previous sentence to exemplify the point.

DC   IC

When it began to rain, we came home.

Because the DC comes before the IC, it is set apart by a comma, which logically follows the Gut Rule: If there is no trauma, don't add a comma. The change in tone comes after the word rain, indicating that the most important information comes thereafter. But, there is no change in tone between the word when and the word it. Generally speaking, if the dependent clause comes before the subject of the IC, set it off, but, if the DC is integrated into the structure of the IC, as in the previous example, leave it alone, unless it is an afterthought. Here, there is a trauma after rain, so we do add a comma. Trauma is the gross disruption of continuity in stress.

When using the colon to express extremely important information, I equate using the colon with using the palms of your hands to slap someone in the chest. It's like saying, "Hey! Listen up!" I always give the analogy of two small children playing at school. However, one is a bully, and he begins to pick on the other one, thinking the smaller one will not fight back. The smaller one, knowing he must completely surprise the bigger, pushes him with both hands as hard as he possibly can, thereby getting the complete attention of the bully. The principle is the same. The colon calls attention to the word or phrase after it.

I only want one thing: Money!

She is only one thing: a user.

He only wanted to go one place: home.

It is permitted to capitalize money in the first example, but it is uncommon to use this construction. However, don't capitalize the other similar constructions, unless they carry enough weight to have an exclamation point at the end of the sentence. The colon stands in direct contrast to the dash in the comparison of importance.

Dash

Use the dash to set off something in the sentence that is unimportant. The item set off, then, is only extra information, and, accordingly, if it were left out of any of these sentences in a composition, the reader would not lose anything important.

> Walking to the store—any day—is relaxing.
>
> I bought a scarf—a green one.
>
> A little boy—one with glasses—fell down on his bike.

We could say that a dash is better suited to use with unimportant interjections than any other kind of punctuation.

Apostrophes

Apostrophes are used to show possession.

The boy's cat fell off the house.

The girl's coat was left at school.

The team's victory took them to the championship.

All of these are singular, so we have noun + apostrophe + s.

If we have possession of the plural form of a regular noun, the apostrophe is located after the s.

Noun + s + apostrophe.

The boys' dog died. (The dog belonged to more than one boy.)

The teams' losses sent them all home. (More than one team lost.)

The computers' abilities nowadays are astounding. (The many abilities of many kinds of different computers astound me.)

Possessive of Irregular Nouns

The children's toys were lost. (The toys that belonged to two or more children were lost.)

"Children" is the plural of child; therefore, the pattern follows that used to make the possessive of a singular noun.

I saw Jesus's picture. There is only one Jesus here, so we follow the rule for a singular noun: It is a singular noun.

I saw the Avants' house. Avants is a family name, plural in this sentence. This means the house that belongs to all of the people in the Avants family. However, if I am only talking about one person named Avants, and only one person lives at that house, I use the pattern for a singular noun, regardless of the -s on the end of the noun.

That is Avants's house. It belongs to Luke Avants.

Apostrophe with a Plural Phrase

There are basically two ways to make this kind of phrase possessive. They are both correct.

That is John's and Tom's cat. (It belongs to both of them.)

That is John and Tom's cat. (It belongs to both of them.)

Sentence Fragments

The most common mistake with fragments is simply not attaching an afterthought to an independent clause.

I went to the store. <u>After the game</u>. WRONG!

OR

<u>After the game</u>. I went to the store. WRONG!

As we mentioned earlier, it must be able to stand alone, in good form, and be a grammatically complete structure, to be an independent clause. A sentence fragment like this is like a grown kid. He is big enough to do what he wants, but he always comes home and asks for money; therefore, he is not actually independent at all. That is the way these fragments appear to you when you read your own material, especially immediately after you complete the assignment. So, when you proofread your papers, see if the construction in question can stand alone, without the assistance of any other sentences around it. If so, you have an independent clause. If not, you have some rewriting to do. If I came up to you, and I said, "After the game," then walked away, you would think I was crazy. Also, when you proofread, read your sentences, the structure, not the ideas. You are too biased to try to read the ideas impartially. If you have any doubts, look to this chapter on punctuation for help. This is also true with papers. You should be able to cut out any given paragraph of a paper, and it should make sense. Therefore, if you begin a paragraph with this or that in reference to something stated in the previous paragraph or if there is no antecedent at all, you have a big problem.

Usually, your reader (the scorer) can easily identify your evidence if you provide transitions in the body of your essay. These transitions act as signals to the reader that you are moving from one point to the next.

Remember: your essays are graded holistically. This means that the reader does not spend time poring over the essay, but rather quickly writes a score based on his initial reading. Simply put, then, your essay should have mile markers that guide the reader from one point to the next. This leads us to the topic of transitions.

CHAPTER THREE:

Transitions

Transitional phrases are what give your essays coherence. They guide the reader from point A to point B. The reader gives your essay a very fast read, quickly scoring in accordance with the first impression of what you wrote. Consequently, the scorer does not have time to stop and think about the topic or mull over any points you have tried to make. S/he simply reads and scores. It is that simple. Look at the lists below. These are transitional phrases that you can memorize and keep in your arsenal for the test.

AGREEMENT: also, plus, in addition, further, furthermore, moreover, additionally, to add to that, next, in accordance with, accordingly, in agreement, finally, for instance, for example, in exemplification, exemplifying that, in fact, factually speaking, in terms of, and so forth, looking at the nexus between, in coordination with, along those lines, collectively speaking, generally speaking, indeed, undoubtedly, obviously, to be sure

CONTRAST: however, contrastingly, in contrast, on the contrary, on the other hand, To put it into perspective, from a different angle, nonetheless, nevertheless, but, yet, a catch to this is, sadly enough, as a hindrance, looking at the holdups, oddly enough, instead, in direct opposition, still, and rather.

RESULT: as a result, as a consequence, consequently, thus, therefore, hence, thereby, resulting in, ultimately, in the end, finally, in the overall analysis, in hindsight, in retrospect, retrospectively, vicariously, the long term effect, as a short term result, significantly, as a major effect, effectively, heretofore, hereafter, thereafter, in short, generally, over all, concluding

I would like to convey a word of caution before we move on. You have only a limited amount of time on your writing assessment sections, so be concise and to the point. The transitional phrases are not to be employed in order to sound pedantic but to provide coherence in your argument.

CHAPTER FOUR

Analysis of Argument

The successful analysis of an argument depends on one's ability to recognize patterns in a written piece. Usually, in formal writing, an author develops an argument by using a specific method to write an essay. These methods are called patterns of development. Although numerous patterns exist, the GRE arguments you analyze will probably be written in the patterns of development below. This is good news, because you basically have three steps: First, recognize the pattern of development; second, identify the flaw in the argument, and finally, analyze the flaw.

Before we look at the patterns of development, beware of the following definitions. "Argument" simply refers to persuasive writing. Writing argument, then, means that a writer is trying to convince the reader to believe something. In addition, the term "flaw" in this context is equivalent to a weak point in a writer's logic or in his pattern of development. The test-taker must identify the flaw and write about that. However, a flaw may not actually be in a writer's argument. You can address the coherence in one's argument if you agree with what you read. Let's look at the patterns of development.

CHAPTER FIVE

Patterns of Development

COMPARISON-CONTRAST: The features or benefits of two items are analyzed, perhaps with particular emphasis on how they differ. To compare is to discuss likenesses, and to contrast is to mention differences.

DEFINITION: The definition pattern usually includes a popular idea of what something is plus one's (the author's) personal concept. Sometimes, this pattern is called "extended definition," because the author goes past the normal idea of what something is (or isn't) to include a personal definition, as well.

CAUSE-EFFECT: The cause-effect pattern can be difficult to recognize at times in that one could simply discuss the effect of something without giving due thought to how a situation developed over a long period of time. For example, one could make a blanket statement such as "Racism exists predominantly in the South due to the higher presence of ex-slave-states there as in contrast to the North." Although this statement may be partially true, the flaw in the argument surfaces, because the writer fails to address other factors that also had a significant influence in the growth of racism in the South. This is what you as the test-taker need to write about. Remember this: If the cause-effect pattern exists, but it is hard to recognize, the writer has failed to make logical connections from beginning to end. That causes a logical fallacy. We'll see those below shortly.

The patterns of development require certain elements to formulate a coherent argument. Without coherence, the points seem to fall apart and the whole argument falls short of persuasion. Yet, at times, an argument may seem to be convincing. Our job as readers is to find the weak spot in the analysis. This is where logical fallacies come in. A logical fallacy is something that appears to be true but in reality is not. An argument based on a logical fallacy is actually based on a flaw.

CHAPTER SIX

Logical Fallacies

Non Sequitur

This Latin phrase means "does not follow." Usually a conclusion does not match the statements before it, or the data does not support the conclusion.

John loves children; He would be a good teacher.

John's love of children does not mean that he would be able to communicate effectively.

False Analogy

An analogy is a comparison of two things that have some sort of similarity, but are dissimilar in other respects. A false analogy is flawed, because it assumes similarity in most other respects. This is where the phrase comparing "apples and oranges" comes from.

If we can build weapons of mass destruction, we should be able to wipe out disease.

Building weapons of mass destruction and wiping out disease are both situations rooted in science, but the obstacles faced with overcoming disease are entirely different from those of building weapons.

Either/Or Fallacy

The either/or fallacy oversimplifies a complex situation to a two-sided argument. Usually, the writer draws a line whereby the reader must accept all or none of the reasoning the writer sets forth.

The government has two choices regarding the budget for next year: either cut the defense spending or people will go hungry.

The either/or fallacy creates a false dilemma. A problem with many alternatives is usually reduced to only two choices.

Circular Reasoning

The conclusion and the support are the same with this logical flaw. The supporting evidence should lead to a logical conclusion, but, with circular reasoning, the conclusion simply restates a claim or the evidence.

A genius has a high IQ, because he is smart.

The second part simply restates the first.

Begging the Question

This type of fallacy is built on a supposition. The foundation of an argument is hypothetical. These fallacies are fairly easy to spot, because they start with phrases like "Let's suppose. . . " or "If x is true, then we could say that y would follow. . . ." You should attack these in argument questions.

Ad Hominem

This phrase literally means "toward the man." It is a ploy to deflect attention away from an issue by attacking its supporter.

> **Senator John Doe's tax plan will fail, because Senator Doe admitted to adultery.**

The attention to the tax plan is drawn away and directed toward Senator Doe. Senator Doe's adultery is not relevant to the tax plan.

Bandwagon Appeal

This device appeals to the reader's sense of belonging, claiming that one should buy into a certain idea because of its popularity. In other words, if 70% of the people believe something, it must be right.

> **70% of the people surveyed agree that Brand X is the best drink in America.**

This is a tactic that tries to make a person feel alienated if s/he disagrees with an issue or an argument. Most often, public opinion is involved in the statement.

Hasty Generalization

This is the same thing as stereotyping. It involves lumping a group of people into the same category because of the characteristics of a few.

Math majors are geeks, because my friend was a math major and he was the biggest geek I have ever known.

The hasty generalization is certainly not limited to people, but it can also include any type of unfair categorization.

CHAPTER SEVEN

Inductive vs. Deductive Logic

Deduction and induction are two methods of presenting evidence in an argument. Deductive logic deals with a supposition that makes a statement and then leads away from it. Induction states many small points and brings forth an answer. The distinction in the argument essay is very clear: The deductive argument generally relies on a leap of faith that is not supported by enough evidence. So, when analyzing the argument, you should look for a flaw in the jump or the leap from the evidence to the conclusion.

> **Overweight people are normally the ones in danger of having heart disease. Tom is a slender man. He is not in any danger of having heart disease.**

The first two statements may be true, yet the conclusion relies on a huge leap of faith. For all we know, Tom could eat three pounds of saturated fat per day. If the conclusion were to read "Tom may not be in danger of having heart disease if he leads a healthy lifestyle," then the conclusion matches the first two statements. The conclusion was qualified by the last clause and so the logic is not flawed.

Look closely at the argument and the wording the question employs. Ensure the reasoning is sound. If not, focus on the errors of the argument when you address the statements.

The inductive argument is the basis of scientific reasoning. Numerous points lead up to a conclusion. For the short essay, inductive logic works best. Whether you are analyzing an error in logic or a well-constructed argument, you should always first address the argument through your thesis statement. Then, your support should be stated in. the body. Analysis of sample questions is certainly crucial at this point.

CHAPTER EIGHT

Sample Argument Questions and Essays

Argument

"Previous experience has shown that soldiers' wives are happiest in areas where residents are highly concerned with leading lives built around the family. We should therefore build our next new military base in a suburb, which has many such residents. Many suburban merchants report that sales of family oriented recreational vehicles are much higher in suburban areas than in metropolitan areas. Further, most often children from a military family tend to join the military like their parent(s) did before them."

Answer:

The conclusion that the next new military base should be built in a suburb is based on inadequate evidence. The writer has a gap in his logic where he supposes that soldiers' wives would be happier living in a suburb than they would be living in a city. His conclusion does not follow his supporting statements.

The author makes two specific errors in his reasoning. Primarily, he stereotypes the people in the city by indicating the wives are happiest in a family-oriented area (No mention of suburb was made). Immediately afterward, the writer claims, "We should therefore build . . . in a suburb." To say that the government should build in a suburb in order to make the wives happy suggests a couple of things. It says that if the wives are happy, the husbands, who presumably are the soldiers, will be happy, as well. The way the statements are set up also implies that suburb would be the most likely place that the wives would be happy and vicariously then the husbands would be happy, too. These implications go a step further: they suggest that city people are less happy, do not build their lives around their families, or do not care for their families as much as suburbanites do. That sets up an either/or logical problem, in which case the reader is pushed into accepting one alternative or the other. Here, the alternatives would be either to build in the suburb as. suggested and therefore be happy or be unhappy with any other possibility. In any of these situations, the writer's points fail. He gives inadequate support to make any of these assumptions. The only evidence given in support of the writer's suggestion to build in the suburb regards the sales of recreational vehicles. Higher sales of family-oriented recreational vehicles in suburban areas could be attributed to many factors. For example, maybe costs of recreational vehicles are cheaper in the suburbs as opposed to the cost of the vehicles in metropolitan areas. In fact, urbanites could even go to the suburbs to buy these vehicles, and that could cause the rise in sales. So, these figures could be misleading. Likewise, the term recreational vehicle may even refer to things like motorcycles, three wheelers, dune buggies, and mini scooters, the likes of which one almost needs to be in the country to be able to drive. Many factors influence these types of figures. Some final comments are in order.

One cannot conclude that people may be happier in the suburbs simply because recreational vehicles sell there more frequently than in the metropolitan areas. The logic is flawed. In addition, the writer has set up two groups of people that are not necessarily in opposition to each other: the city people and the suburbanites. Overall, the reasoning overlooks some vital information, and that destroys its soundness.

Argument

The following appeared in a letter sent by a group of concerned parents from the Academy private school to all of the school board members.

"Two years ago, students in nearby Hampton community instituted a set of rules on how the students should dress. Since then, the incidence of violence on private campus has decreased by 30%. We should adopt our own set of restrictions on how our students should dress at school."

Answer:

The letter includes an incident of faulty cause and effect reasoning. The parents err in the supposed connection that they have made between the change in student dress and the decrease in violence on campus. Their logic will not bear much scrutiny.

For whatever the reason that the Hampton community sought to impose a dress code on the students, the outcome was certainly not visibly linked to the decrease in violent behavior. Basically, we only have two facts to deal with: the uniforms were required, and the violence went down on campus. There could be another connection involved that we as readers are not aware of. As the parents' claim stands, the rules on student dress led directly to the change in student behavior. Too much has been left unsaid. There is a fact that needs consideration. The school was a private school, and usually private schools do not have the same problems that public schools do that are cured by instituting uniforms. For example, if violence had occurred between warring gangs whose members wore certain colors, the removal of those colors could possibly have a positive effect, like described here with the private school. This line of reasoning given implies that one thing caused the other, primarily because the decrease followed the rule for wearing a uniform. That is the classic case of the logical fallacy "post hoc ergo propter hoc." The phrase translates: "After this therefore because of this." Too many other aspects come into play that could affect the reasoning, as well. As a result, wearing the required uniform may only coincide with the reduction of violence. Other factors are never mentioned that could figure heavily into the problems on campus. If fights were more frequent in the hotter months of the year, for instance, the uniform certainly would not reduce the flare of tempers that normally accompany springtime. But, if the uniforms just happen to come along at the right time, this could make all the difference in the world in the appearance of a cause-effect relationship between the fall in violence and uniforms. Along those lines, we do not know if the uniforms were required in October, hypothetically, when the weather is cool in many places, and the hormones of teenagers stay in their proper place or if the uniforms came out in late August. Other causes like threats from the coaches to bench players, students' failure in classes, and other disciplinary actions on the part of the administration stemming from fighting could be responsible for more acceptable student behavior. We can't fail to recognize that one remedy to a problem usually comes with several other remedies. Consequently, we can't look at the parents' one cause and accept that as the ONLY cause. Too many factors are left unseen to make a blanket statement that defies logic. I need to make some final comments.

Reasonable people know that most often events appear to cause other events when they both occur around the same time. This is the case here. The parents' argument lacks coherence, because no clear connection exists.

Argument

The following appeared in a magazine article about graduates in the city of Boston.

"In Boston, the number of business school graduates who went to work for large firms declined by 10 percent over the last five years, but an increasing number of graduates took jobs at small firms. Even though large firms usually offer much higher salaries, business graduates are choosing to work for the smaller firms most likely because the graduates experience greater job satisfaction at smaller firms. In a survey of graduating students at a leading business school, most indicated that job satisfaction was more important than making a high salary. This suggests that the larger firms of Boston will need to offer graduates more benefits and other incentives and reduce the employees' workload."

Answer:

The line of reasoning above is sound in one respect but flawed in the conclusion. The writer indicates that number of graduates going to work for the bigger companies has declined by 10% but those working for the smaller firms increased. The soundness of the logic centers on the students' own admission that they wanted job satisfaction as compared to a higher salary. This leads to a jump in logic to the conclusion that bigger companies can lure the new graduates with more money and less time at work. These points warrant more discussion.

The decrease in the number of graduates going to work for larger companies that pay a high salary as opposed to smaller companies with a lower salary certainly goes hand in hand with the students search for job satisfaction. Most students surveyed actually said they wanted more enjoyment at work, and the numbers indicate they sought this out in smaller firms. In fact, that caused a decrease in the number of people going to work for the better paying companies. Apparently, the supposition of the author has been proven further by a period of five years of decrease in graduates' employment at bigger firms. This evidence certainly lends credence and validity to the author's claim about job satisfaction. Yet, a problem still exits with his conclusion. The author states that bigger firms will need to "offer graduates more benefits and other incentives and reduce the employees' workload" to attract them. I called this a jump in logic for several reasons. The students said they wanted job satisfaction and not a higher salary. The writer of the article goes back to the very thing that is currently offered. He says very clearly that "benefits and other incentives" may attract the graduates. This is illogical, because it has little to do with job satisfaction. According to the author, the students indicated that "job satisfaction was more important than making a high salary." The author has attempted to shift the emphasis from money to benefits. Yet, and more importantly, money does not equal job satisfaction. One cannot equate the two. This needs qualification, however. The author has thrown a red herring into the argument. The benefits, incentives, and a reduced workload seem to fall under a different definition than higher salary, and they probably are defined differently in most cases if they are not cash or cash equivalent. This red herring, which is designed to throw the reader off track of why graduates are avoiding big business, still does not answer the question that most graduates need answered in order to come to corporate America: How can one get job satisfaction in big business? Therefore, the writer's argument, as cleverly written as it may be, fails. The challenge still remains for big business: make the job satisfying to this percentage of new graduates. This deserves some final thoughts. The author makes a good point about new graduates and why they are leaving the promise of a higher salary in bigger business firms. S/he even backs up the claim with a survey. However, the answer is never fully explained by the author as to how one can get job satisfaction. S/he simply threw in a red herring logical fallacy to mask the failure to provide an answer.

Argument

The following appeared in an advertisement for a candidate of the Atkins town council.

"In the next town council election, residents of Atkins should vote for Joe Johns, who is a member of the Clean Air Group, rather than for Bob Rowe, a member of the Atkins town council, because the current members are not protecting our environment. For example, during the past year the number of factories in Atkins has doubled, air pollution levels have increased, and the local clinic has treated 25 percent more patients with breathing ailments. If we elect Joe Johns, the pollution problems in Atkins will certainly be solved."

Answer:

The preceding argument has two flaws in logic. First, there is a problem with the cause-effect analysis with the air pollution. Second, the writer attacks the council members thereby drawing attention away from the issue of qualifications of Joe Johns, the writer's candidate. These points require further observation.

The author claims that the current council members are responsible for several problems that exist in the community and that is why the incumbent candidate should not be re-elected. The writer states that "the number of factories . . . have doubled, air pollution has increased, and the local clinic has treated 25% more patients with breathing ailments." All of these problems are wrongly attributed to the current town council. These things are not necessarily the effects of the action or inaction of the town council. There is not a clear link between the cause-effect patterns that the writer suggests exists. Further, we could divide these items and analyze to make a distinction between each. Factories are generally considered a sign of progress, a source of jobs and therefore revenue for the community. We do not have any information that implies the factories cause any type of pollution. These new factories could be chicken processing plants for all we know as readers. Those two points fail. The writer errs in the nexus between the breathing ailments and air pollution. There is no information given as to the nature of the breathing ailments. The cause could be seasonal allergies that have an effect on respiration or even asthma problems. This leads to the ad hominem attack the writer employs to draw attention to the so-called problems caused by the town council and divert attention away from the qualifications of Joe Johns, the writer's favorite candidate. The writer never tells us why Joe Johns would be an effective town council member. The writer only implies that Mr. Johns' membership in a local environmental group should be qualification enough to address the demands of the council position. This ad hominem attack (meaning toward the person) is a favorite diversionary tactic that relies on smearing an individual to divert attention away from a different topic. This exactly what the writer has done. I must finally mention that the author in closing makes one last unsubstantiated claim. The author states that with the election of Joe Johns, the pollution problem in Atkins would "certainly be solved." There is no support for that or any other such claim.

The author has diverted attention away from the issue of qualification in a couple of ways. First, a cause-effect relationship has muddled the issue with the creation of supposed problems. Second, the attack on character relies on the mud slinging most people expect in politics. The writer's scenario fails, however, due to inadequate support.

Argument

The following appeared in a letter written from a supervisor to the administrator of a teaching hospital where both were employed.

"Ten years ago, the teaching hospital set into motion a new program that allowed students to evaluate the teaching effectiveness of all their supervisors. Since then, hospital supervisors have begun to give higher scores in student evaluations, and overall student grade averages at the hospital have risen by about twenty percent. Other teaching hospitals apparently believe the grades at the teaching hospital are inflated; this could indicate why our teaching hospital graduates have not been as successful at gaining full-time employment compared to graduates from nearby University Hospital. To enable its graduates to secure better jobs, the teaching hospital should now terminate student rating of teaching hospital supervisors."

Answer:

The dean that wrote the letter has an illogical sequence in his causal chain. He indicates the students receive higher grades, because they can evaluate supervisors, and, as a result of this, other potential employers do not hire the graduates. This seems like a plausible argument at first glance, but, upon closer scrutiny, it falls apart. Let's view its components more closely.

It is certainly possible that students perceived as having inflated grades may not be hired as quickly as those students they are in competition with, especially if the grades have risen by about 20%. Yet, the writer goes a step further and proposes to discontinue student evaluation of supervisors. He says, "To enable its graduates to secure better jobs, the teaching hospital should now terminate student rating of . . . supervisors." One can fairly easily see that the writer makes a leap of faith if we turn the sentence around. It would look like this: "terminating student rating of supervisors would enable the teaching hospital graduates to secure better jobs. This is where the writer errs in his logical sequence. One must recall that the supposed grade inflation was a possible hindrance to the graduates' hiring with other local employers; therefore, the immediate discontinuation of student rating would not necessarily have any impact at all on the graduates' employability or even the actual hiring. This is true for several reasons. First, the stigma would still remain with the students–if indeed that were a factor to begin with. Second, it could take months or even years to overcome the stigma and return to normalcy. Third, the comparison of employability that the dean provided was to the students at University hospital, whose hiring rate was higher than graduates of teaching hospital. We have no information on the students from the University hospital. The school there could have better programs. Their students may receive training for formal interviews. The students may indeed be better qualified. Finally, the students themselves from the teaching hospital could lack the background necessary to succeed or even compete for that matter. The argument the dean provides is fraught with numerous contingencies. Some final comments are in order.

For one to give such an overwhelmingly pat answer to such a monstrous problem as weak employability takes root in serious logical problems. The sequence presupposes an outcome that relies on too many links in the chain. As a result, the argument is too weak to be logically sound.

Argument

The following appeared in a memo from the director of the town of Red Rock Quarry.

"Two years ago, our game and fish speculators predicted that the gravel pit which is used for discarding old timber that residents have dug up and have no place to put would be completely filled within five years. During the past two years, however, area residents have been reusing wood products much more than anticipated for mulch, heating, and building purposes.

Next month, the amount of material recycled should further increase, because the weather is getting colder. In addition, over fifty percent of the respondents to a recent survey said that they use wood products for heating purposes in the future. Because of the people's promise to reuse the wood products, the available space in our gravel pit should last for considerably longer than expected."

Answer:

The chain of events appears credible, at least in the beginning. However, the writer is somewhat quick to jump to a conclusion regarding the end result. Bluntly stated, he has taken a couple of small events and made a big leap of faith. Let's take a closer look to see how the first several items do not necessarily lead to the conclusion stated.

The director has errantly taken the following three items as the basis of his conclusion, which is that the gravel pit would last longer (as a landfill) than the originally thought period of five years. First, he states that area residents have reused the wood products more than expected for the past two years, so the pit is not now as full as it should be. Second, the director speculates that citizens may even use more wood than that for heat due to oncoming cold weather. Third, he relies on the residents' statements indicating they would use wood for heat in the future. For succinctness, let's view each point again individually. First, the director cannot rely on the increase in recycling over the past two years as a prediction for the next three years' activity. Any number of factors could have influenced that particular statistic that we simply are unaware of. Further, weighing that statistic against the original projection of conservation speculators seems highly unwise. One could be assured that conservation speculators had had a wider range of factors and statistics from which to make their conclusion than the director had. Therefore, point one appears to be too weak to be a basis for any prediction. Point two in and of itself is not a bad bet, but in this case, it is not weighty enough to be logically sound-at least in relation to the director's ultimate conclusion. People may use more wood during the colder months. That is a given. However, the amount they use is probably negligible in comparison to the rest of the year. Further, perhaps a milder winter could be forthcoming. This is too speculative to be used as a foundation. Finally, the people's claim that they will use additional wood in the future has little relevance. Additional wood does not mean more wood than normal: it means they will continue to use wood. The people simply said, "Yes, we will use wood." That is all. These deserve some closing observations.

The three points together only appear to make a sound case. Analyzed separately, though, they do not make a logical progression. One could say that the conclusion does not line up with the supporting evidence.

Argument

The following appeared in a letter from the owner of AAA Home Builders' Supply, a small business serving a suburban town.

"Evidence suggests that people are becoming more and more interested in doing their own home improvements themselves. A national survey conducted last month indicated that many consumers were no longer willing to pay the price that private contractors require for most home improvement. And locally, the do it yourself magazines have sold out at the local bookstore for the past several months. Therefore, we at AAA Home Builders' Supply can increase our profits by greatly expanding the variety of home care products we normally keep in stock."

Answer:

Homeowners will frequently try to cut costs in home improvement by doing things themselves, especially if they are so inclined. But, the owner has made a couple of connections based on very limited evidence. He has taken the high volume of sales regarding do it yourself magazines as exemplary of people's desire to do their own work, which does not appear like a logical conclusion. In addition, he assumes that he can cash in on what he presumes will be a trend in the market by citing evidence of high magazine sales. The three points don't really line up.

People's refusal to pay high prices to private contractors certainly appears to be a good foundation for the owner's reasoning. After all, if people need to have improvements done on their home and they refuse to pay the contractor, perhaps the next logical solution would be to do the work themselves. This is not necessarily so. Other alternatives are out there. Homeowners could choose to pay a friend or a relative to do the work. These workers are usually referred to as shade-tree mechanics, at least if they are working on cars. A shade-tree carpenter might even try to cut costs himself by using secondhand materials. So, they wouldn't be so quick to run down and buy new products like the owner is hoping. Furthermore, homeowners may not even have the work done. They may decide to wait. That doesn't explain away the high magazine sales, though. No explanation is really necessary for that. People may be thinking about doing something, but, as I said, never act on it. Incidentally, the magazines' high sales could have been for one specific item or one seasonal promotion. For example, if the summer were nearing (we have no information either way), people could be thinking about swimming pools. Those magazines sometimes include things one purchases without constructing. Buyers may have been eyeing items like these. Too many factors interfere with the cause and effect that the owner is acting on. That leads to the final point, a proposal really, that the owner makes. He claims he can increase sales in his store if he expands his variety of products. That expansion, of course, keys right into the magazine sales. He could possibly increase his sales if he were to expand his line of products. There is no guarantee, however. Spending his hard earned money based on an increase in magazine sales is quite a drastic move.

The owner is all too eager to look at a national survey, hear some opinions, and then jump to a couple of conclusions. In the middle of these points, numerous factors could offset what he hopes will happen nd that is make more money. All in all, the owner takes the national survey, looks at a very small area, and links the two, making a couple of connections that seem somewhat out of sequence. He has too much at stake to jump in with his argument.

Argument

The following appeared in the minutes recorded in the Boone County Commissioners annual meeting.

"Boone County recently lowered its speed limit from 70 miles per hour to 55 on all major county roads in an attempt to improve highway safety. However, the 70 mph limit should be reinstituted, because this change has been relatively insignificant. Most drivers are exceeding the new speed limit, and the accident rate throughout Boone County has decreased only slightly. Boone County should find an alternative, such as increasing law enforcement presence. Our neighbor, Dent County increased law enforcement, and this has had a tremendous effect on the traffic safety in the area. Dent County roads still have a 70 mph speed limit, but there were 20 percent fewer reported accidents in Dent County this past year than there were five years ago when law enforcement was increased."

Answer:

The link between the speed limit and traffic safety is one that normally speaks for itself, but here, the verdict is not really in yet on the effect on the reduction of the speed limit and traffic safety, because too many other variables are involved in the equation. Factors such as amount of time the reduction has been in place, locale of people's speeding in disregard of the new speed limit, and incomplete data for Dent County make the analogy to Dent County statistics rather inconclusive. Looking at them separately should give a little more insight into the subject.

Beginning drivers are usually taught that the one sure way to take control of one's safety while driving is to slow down. Reducing the speed limit from 70 mph to 55 should be a safety factor. The minutes say that the speaker feels that the 70 mph should be reinstated for two reasons: 1) Drivers still speed. 2) The decrease in accidents has been slight. For a speeder, or at least one who feels inconvenienced by the new 55 mph speed limit, those are presented as good reasons, and in any other circumstances, they could well be good reasons for the reinstatement of the 70 mph limit. In this circumstance, however, these two reasons just aren't enough to act on—at least not yet. In that driver safety is of paramount importance, we need to see why not. Foremost, there is no indication given as to how long the 55 mph limit has been in effect. Ample time should be given for the people to actually react to the new law. Breaking the people's habit of driving 70 mph could take a little while. If the new limit had only been in effect a couple of weeks at the time the minutes above were written, this idea would certainly be applicable. In addition, the data on wrecks may take a long time to be processed. So, no news in this situation could be good news. Receiving the reports just takes time. By holding out a little longer, the board may see that the data supports a lower limit. Again, these are details that are not provided. That brings us to the comparison to Dent County. Dent County may only be comparable in part. We only know that Dent County had a decrease in accidents (reported), and they hired more police officers. One could be relatively accurate in saying that people will slow down around policemen. Hiring more policemen following Dent County's example sounds like an outstanding proposition. If people will slow down around policemen and be under a lower speed limit, the accidents, speeding tickets, and generally unsafe driving may all be reduced. The points here are better viewed as a combination rather than an either/or proposal.

The facts do take a little time to come in when the subject involves changing people's driving habits. Further, no mention of the time frame in Boone County was ever made. As a result, the commissioners should not be too hasty to generalize regarding the information they do have. The analogy to Dent County does give some useful information, but adding to that ensures a higher level of safety. Saving lives, after all, is the commission's top priority.

CHAPTER NINE

Analysis of Issue

The issue analysis is a measure of one's ability to look at an issue from every perspective. It revolves around looking at a complicated issue effectively and relating to the facets of an issue in a precise manner. This does include your opinions, and you need to respond cogently and coherently, using supporting evidence to substantiate any claims you may make in your essay. If a question contains more than one side or alternative, explore each. Remember: this portion of the test centers on your ability to look at an issue, relate it to the surrounding context, and weigh it against any other factors involved in the question.

Pattern of Development

In order to write effective paragraphs, one needs to present the essay in a specific pattern of development. It is highly unwise to sit down and simply start writing. A pattern of development is the method one uses to write an essay. They are fairly simple to learn and can make all the difference in the world in the score on an essay. Generally speaking, an essay question will determine the way a reader responds in an essay question. The content is not determined, but the pattern of development usually is. This means that you can look at the way a question is worded and choose the best pattern of development to employ. Sometimes, the wording of a question may allow more than one pattern of development in a response. I would not mix the patterns of development. For example, I would determine that a question is best answered in a comparison-contrast pattern and proceed from there as opposed to mixing the comparison-contrast with a cause-effect pattern. Your essay answer will be short enough that you will only employ one pattern effectively.

The question will usually contain certain words that signal a certain type of response. Again, the questions only affect your method of response rather than the content of the response itself. Let's look at some patterns of development that are normally employed in writing essays.

CHAPTER TEN

Comparison-Contrast

In the Comp-Contrast paper, look for words that suggest a relationship of similarity or dissimilarity. They may be words like opposite, alike, unlike, in common, or any other words with the same meanings. Be aware of signals that will give you ideas on how to address the topic. The ease that a reader takes in a pattern of development is based in the ability to move back and forth from point to point, comparing each in a relatively short time. This is good for him, but the writing of the point-by-point pattern of development usually takes longer for the student. However, on the exam, the points are there

tively easy to write out. Therefore, I suggest the point-by-point pattern for exams, especially if the exam is only three to four paragraphs in length. This involves stating opposing items in every other sentence. The GRE Issue Analysis would normally be best written at a four to five paragraph length. Consequently, you need to have a certain approach in the introduction. Let's say that your response to an issue has three main points you want to cover. If so, you need to have five sentences in the introduction. They include the 1) thesis statement 2) evidentiary statement #1 3) evidentiary statement #2 4) evidentiary statement #3 5) the transitional sentence that exits the introduction. They call for closer observation.

The ES, which stands for evidentiary statement, is the sentence that provides evidence to support your Th.S. or thesis statement. Following, though, despite only having one paragraph in the body, we have two evidentiary statements. This is a rare exception, and it is usually common with a point-by-point pattern in an essay where the two topics are dealt with in the body of the essay together. It is commonly called an ABAB pod, because every sentence jumps back to the subject. For example, one sentence is about A and the next is about B. This allows the reader to compare the two items fairly well without loss of time, which is important to a grader who does a lot of reading.

Let's look at a point-by-point pod that deals with a tangible subject. Plus, the transitionals will be highlighted, so you can see exactly how to glue the ideas together. First, look at the diagram below. With a point-by-point pod, you can basically look at the possibilities in several ways. Primarily, with a really short paper, the A-B, A-B, A-B, A-B style works, but it fails if you have a longer paper, say around four to five pages typed. Plus, we do not want to have a singsong rhythm that becomes monotonous. This style may still work, but we can apply it to one topic, perhaps encompassing 4-5 sentences. You make the decision about the length.

The first example of this type of paper is set up in the following format: AAABBB. The sentences should be equally grouped. For now, look over the next paper. Note the places I have written notes to you. I have highlighted the transitionals, so you can observe how we manipulate our sentence structure, reader attention, and the focus on the content. Of course, this is a simple example, but we will certainly see this type of pattern employed with more difficult, sample questions later.

CHAPTER ELEVEN

Sample Patterns of Development Comparison-Contrast

For the individual who puts stock in the old and traditional, the strength of foundation, and the grandeur of space, the traditional house may be the choice of a lifetime.[ES1] The motifs of style that have long been played out in today's market of prefabricated homes are existent in those structures of that were popular in the past. In addition,[ES2] foundations were stronger in older houses, and they still are, even given the course of time. For whatever reason,[ES3] older homes also tend to be larger. These points certainly warrant more discussion.

Reader: Now, you can write the body two separate ways with point-by-point pattern of development. First, you can write the sentences in a point by point- one sentence about A, and one about B, until you complete the category. Secondly, you can group the sentences together that pertain to ES1, evidentiary statement number one, which is the same statement that you made which supports the thesis statement. Therefore, the first motif of style could be written about in the following manner.

Note: Indentation indicates the start of a new paragraph, which typically includes the indentation or space of five letters. A space is the size of a letter. Please note that the letters A and B are only written here to show how the sentences go back and forth between the two points. In addition, the sentences are only separated for clarity, and no paragraph should be written in that structure of indentation. We will see how the structure changes on sample questions and answers following these paragraphs, which only introduce patterns.

The style of older structures carries the charm of aristocracy or the peace of the rustic countryside as compared to the assembly-like packaging of modern homes.

A. <u>Basically</u>, the shopper has the variety from which to choose in the market of older structures.

A. <u>For instance</u>, if one wants to enjoy the old world of the nineteenth century, he can search in the "second-hand" market.

A. <u>Moreover</u>, the buyer can choose from different time periods, haggle on prices, or even negotiate in the arena of remodeling.

B. <u>On the other hand</u>, modern homes of today are thrown together in a hurry, many having the same features.

B. <u>Along those lines</u>, most homes in a particular subdivision cost about the same, so variety is limited.

B. <u>Consequently</u>, if the buyer wants to stand out in the crowd, the modern home disallows much personal freedom.

Reader: You should see how the underlined phrases tie the ideas together, provide contrast among the points, and ultimately guide the reader. However, we could have set up the body's format in one paragraph with the alternating ABAB method. That leads us into a different type of pattern: the cause-effect.

CHAPTER TWELVE

Cause-Effect

Lifting weights can have a comprehensive effect on one's well being. One may very well experience an immediate difference in endurance, leading to an increase in appetite, in turn fighting off sickness through good diet, and culminating in marked levels of strength. Often, beginners say they feel increased energy throughout the day. The relationships between food, feeling, and appearance are inseparable. After time, those same people love to look in the mirror, because the positive gains are surely noticeable. This is information that certainly needs to be shared.

Lifting weights has so many positive results, but one that is shocking to many people is how quickly a person improves his energy levels. For instance, in as little as two weeks, the average Joe can significantly increase his ability to last. That means more energy at the end of the day. As a result, he could take extra classes at night. A night workout schedule may also take form. Instead of feeling wiped out from a day at work, one could engage in productive things like community service, or even volunteering to help a friend. More importantly, by giving a little of oneself to time out in the gym, a person can experience a return on his investment that can never be measured. Not only does exercise affect the endurance level but also the appetite.

When an athlete, or most anyone for that matter, fuels his body sufficiently and efficiently, his mind and body both reach new levels of competence. The small, pesky cold no longer nags like it did before those cleansing workouts, specifically because the body is cleansed of impurities through life-sustaining nourishment. Anti-oxidants whisk away the toxins in one's system. The blood circulation, as a result, experiences higher levels of oxygen; thus, one has more defensive ability. Hence, the body is hungrier than before, and any fuel, accordingly, might be used to maintain the system's requirements. There is a direct link between exercise, eating, and health.

The single most significant marker for a lot of weight lifters is the ability to make progress in lifting. Most men say that to look in the mirror and see visible differences in the gaining of muscle-mass enhances their performance in the gym. Whether he is conscious about it or not, then, a guy feels better about himself when he can put more weight on the bar. It is no joke to surmise that all of the factors discussed here are inextricably wound up together in one way or another. The more a guy lifts, the stronger he gets. The stronger he gets, the more his body requires fuel. The more fuel he consumes, the more his muscle mass increases. Then, he is drawn to the mirror, and he sees progress with time. The more time he spends, the more gains he sees. The cycle is certainly one big circle.

To have a program is a good idea. To obtain whatever goals one has necessitates planning, commitment, and hard work. The main factor to persistence, many times, is one's ability to visualize what comes next, even though the net result may not be readily apparent. Diligence and visualization are the keys to implementing the cycle of success.

Comment:

At times, you may have to identify an issue that is categorized with other several items. In that case, identify your issue and classify the items. That calls for addressing the elements of each, usually putting particular emphasis on the point you want to stress.

CHAPTER THIRTEEN

Division-
Classification
Sample Paper

All writing falls into two categories: Exposition and Persuasion. Exposition includes periodicals and didactic material which only purpose is to inform. Sometimes, just across a blurred line of distinction sits persuasion, which main purpose is to influence the reader to think a certain way or to do something, and this category includes rhetorical pieces along with a miscellany of others. Sometimes, close scrutiny is required to distinguish exactly where a piece fits.

Periodicals include daily newspapers, monthly magazines, and also quarterlies. Generalizing, we will assume that the primary objective of those that report the news is to inform, and these are the ones we are interested in. Any reputable news reporting agency, following the formal and ethical rules of reporting, tends to be objective, not moralizing or changing the facts. The one end in mind is to report, giving the facts, with no personal stake involved other than to convey the information in an unbiased fashion. Of course, there are some that deviate from this norm, such as tabloid periodicals, but those are not in this class. Texts are good examples of didactic material, that which is used to teach. The author tells the reader something, from a factual perspective, with no personal involvement in the outcome of the information. To qualify that statement, I must add that the author knows the truth, and the reader's acceptance of the information is good. If not, that is fine, too, because the information is generally accepted anyway. The author of a textbook is not trying to convince the reader that the author himself is right. He simply presents the information, and his responsibility is over, assuming his other responsibilities as an educator are fulfilled prior to that. News stories, news broadcasts, weather forecasts, textbooks, encyclopedias, and reports all belong to this category. At times, differentiating between the categories of exposition and persuasion is extremely difficult. The method to categorize material is to question why the information is given. If the presenter benefits according to the belief the reader has in the content of the material, then, the material is probably persuasive, or what is adjectivally referred to as argumentative. Students write an argument through term papers and essays. The most revered argument written in the Age of Reason comes in the form of rhetoric. Rhetorical writing and speech became an art, and they still are, actually. The aim is to persuade the thoughts and influence the actions of the reader and the listener. It involves cadence, assonance, consonance, and figurative language. Traces of these techniques are also seen in places like theses, newspaper editorials, and advertisements. The most skillful professional, however, wants to influence the reader to believe, but without the reader realizing this belief has crept into being. For instance, proposals for big business involve research, perhaps costing millions of dollars. Then, a bid is made to obtain work or something equally beneficial, all with the express goal to achieve an end. Buying a car, for example, is a typical scenario where one may be convinced to buy through imagery and logic. Again, depending on the awareness of the reader or the listener, the consumer is pulled by, pushed from, and exposed to the art of persuasion. Looking at the barrage of what we are exposed to daily hones the skills of judging what we see.

Understanding the fine line that separates exposition and persuasion benefits people every day. The basic understanding emanates from a center of calm when hit by the desire to accept information thrown our way. Not always, but usually, the one throwing out the information reveals why. Like getting to know someone, eventually, it's not hard to observe and make value judgments, ones based in experience and in an informed decision making process.

CHAPTER FOURTEEN:

Definition

The good co-worker can be classified into many categories, but the two main categories are apparent. Obviously, the best co-worker is a helpful person. He is not always a personal and close friend, but he is one who knows how to respect personal space and help when the time calls for it. These necessitate further exploration.

A person can help in a thousand different ways. Those ways do not have to be limited to the 9-5 day either. If one's vehicle is not working satisfactorily, the co-worker could even save the day at just the perfect time. A ride goes a long way in the cold. Moreover, the friendly wave from across the room speaks a lot during a long day at work. A watchful eye around the area keeps work overload to a minimum. At other times, working side by side is called for. The needed tool or some advice is sometimes found at the next desk. These things appear small, but they add up. As it is good to see the friend when in need, it is also good not to see him, too.

Personal space is a luxury that most people cherish. As a result, a worker always wants to see quiet time as quiet time. It can be highly annoying to read something twice. Also, at times, people just do not want to talk. Along those lines, to respect a person's privacy means to know when not to wave, when not to come and ask for a tool, and when not to make conversation. Smart people know when to say no to saying hi. It is not always that easy, but the idea speaks for itself. Some final words may shed more light on the subject.

Around the world, people always deal with good and bad co-workers. Regardless of the cultural differences between people, they usually appreciate help and respect. Though the definitions vary, a good colleague is usually helpful and respectful at the same time. It is all a matter of kindness.

Note To Reader: The paper divides the quality of goodness and classifies the examples into a) helpfulness and b) respect for personal space.

CHAPTER FIFTEEN:

Sample Essay Questions and Answers

We now need to look at some sample, essay questions and some specific answers. Remember: 1) Identify the type of pattern you will respond in. 2) Use support to back up any claims you make.

Question

It is easier to learn from a mentor with whose philosophies you agree as opposed to learning from one with whom you disagree. Opposition can be stressful and thwart the learning process.

Answer:

It may most often be easier in the short run to learn from an individual with whom one gets along and whose philosophies that one shares, but, in the overall scheme of things, that knowledge may discontinue in its growth, because it is not challenged. Growth works on an underlying principle: apply more pressure and grow as a result. Too much agreement can lead to sloth and comfort, perhaps even eventually to atrophy. These points warrant clarification.

Most people might agree that, for a short period of time, they would rather learn from someone whom they admire and with whom have a lot in common. These things lend to the comfort and relaxation that one might like to feel when learning. Yet, as the old proverb goes (paraphrasing), "For learning to continue, the student must become smarter than the teacher." As true as it may be, even in a limited sense, that we usually learn better when we are relaxed, there is a point where learning is acquired through a painful process. The trial and error is a method of learning. The pain that comes from the process is so invaluable that it cannot be measured. Most often, the scientist that goes through this painful process is in the lab alone, without help, without a teacher, without anything but the test tube and his own personal notes. The statement that one may learn more is true, but only to the point where the maxim takes effect and proves true. Learning does progress where and when the student overtakes his teacher. This leads us to the next point. Where exactly does the student decide that he is better off to seek out a teacher or mentor with whom he does not share ideals and philosophies? The answer should be very clear: Where the student wants to overtake his teacher is the point where that claim "It is easier to learn from a mentor with whose philosophies you agree as opposed to learning from one with whose philosophies you disagree" is no more true. Its logic ceases to apply to the new teacher. Several reasons underscore this fact. Primarily, the push toward acquiring knowledge comes from two stimuli: A) One simply wants to know. If one simply wants to know the truth about something, he will continue to look for answers when his mentor can no longer provide them. There need be no conflict. Philosophy has little to do with it. At that point, agreement or disagreement in philosophical issues have no bearing on what one does. B) One wants to prove his worth. This is rooted in pride. Many leaders throughout history have accomplished monumental feats, because others told them it was impossible. These people come from nothing most often. They thrive on stress and questioning, doubt, envy, and everything that goes along with opposition. These are the true overcomers, people like Napoleon and Henry VIII. I need to make a concession, though.

Too much opposition can thwart the progress for many people. Many children need to be nurtured and tenderly brought along in order to bring them to a point that they can think critically. The strength of the West has been in teaching our students to think critically. Yet, they were not given a textbook at seven and told to critique it. They were brought along and taught how to look at things, where to analyze an argument, and why to look for faults in certain reasoning. One cannot hope to perform at a top level in competition without having pressure applied to his ability. This is true with the muscular, skeletal, and the cardiovascular systems. Working through the pressure may not be a delightful process at the time, but the end result makes it worthwhile. The subject needs some closing comments.

The pursuit of knowledge is a very personal experience. This is why some people do like to learn from someone they agree with on almost all issues. Yet, for the student to overtake the teacher, the student should expect opposition. That mentor may not go gentle into that good night as Dylan Thomas once wrote. We should not expect him to, either. To get to that angle of repose though, academically, one needs to be prepared for a lot of opposition and a lot of hard work.

Question

Private schools should be forced to study the same content as all other schools in their classrooms. No deviation should be allowed in any of the school districts.

Answer:

The government should require that all schools follow the same curriculum, at least in part, whether or not the school in question is private or public. All public schools should be under the same mandatory guidelines to ensure the separation of church and state. However, the private schools should be allowed to add to their curriculum in alignment with their right to integrate religious issues with the daily routine, but only insofar as the school is private and meets the some of the same requirements as the public schools. Yet, the common denominator between the two types of schools must be a mandatory national curriculum in order to monitor our children's progress as a whole. Both points certainly gain a little more respect when interfaced with each other.

The public schools should be viewed as an extension of the government's responsibility to accommodate the needs of our youth. By so doing, each child has the same opportunity to pursue happiness and be successful. Many different factors are involved in this pursuit. Primarily, though, for anyone to be able to have the widest range of possibilities, s/he has to have an educational background that opens doors. For everyone to have the same chance, they should be forced, not allowed, to follow the same curriculum as every other individual. If this is not done, the richer school districts will have the best curriculum. Along those lines, the poorer school districts would have the worst curriculum. That could and probably would create a glut of college enrollees from only the richer areas. Then, chaos would ensue. For generations thereafter, the poorer kids would be locked into menial jobs and their children's children after them, right down the line. If everyone follows the same curriculum, that would be a moot point. Even now, poor people can take out government-subsidized loans, so money is usually not a factor. That does not necessarily mean that going to the most expensive colleges like Harvard is an option, but college certainly is within reach. Everyone has the same chance, which is our guarantee in the Constitution. No portion of the national curriculum should be excluded in any school district in the United States. This brings us to the topic of private schools.

Private schools should, however, be able to add to the national curriculum. It is the constitutional right of parents to educate their children as they see appropriate, but they still need to abide by the mandates of the government in regard to the foundational requirements. These requirements can be fulfilled by the national curriculum. This is where the addition of religious education comes into the scenario. Each individual school should be able to determine what to add to the school's curriculum. Then, the best of both possible worlds is always possible: a student can learn what is needed in the eyes of the government and what is also needed in the eyes of the parents. These topics warrant some final thoughts.

Our country has capitalized off the potpourri of different ideas, ethnic groups, and religious ideologies. We have learned to function as an entity that strives amidst diversity. Working together, we have accomplished more than any other culture at any other time in the history of mankind. The elements of diversity and cohesion have worked together to create the superpower status that we now enjoy. Accordingly, we need to continue in the same vein that we have and continue to work toward the common goal of success for all of our citizens. We can attain that goal through a national curriculum, one that is mandatory for public and private schools alike. To maintain our individualism, we also need to have the ability to include our ideology in the course of the school day. Therefore, private schools must be allowed to add to the curriculum required by the state. This way, everyone wins.

Question

The best result in understanding any society comes by studying the habits of its young people.

Answer:

The study of any culture must certainly include the impact of the youth on the society as a whole, but that part of the culture is only a microcosm in the overall structure. The youth should be looked at in terms of a link in a chain. These links come together and change over time, so the whole structure should be analyzed in its growth and stability. Looking at the youth as a link and how the links change over time should shed a little more light on their effects on each other and one's understanding of any society.

The youth have a tremendous effect in any society, especially in seeing how they have the ability to influence marketing trends, fashion, and the automobile industry Young people are no longer seen and not heard. They have a voice in contemporary society. But, they are usually not completely self-sufficient. This dependence on others makes them simply a link in a bigger chain. The economic factor that so many young people fight with to gain independence is the very trait that defines youth. It is because most young people are dependent on others for their subsistence that they cry so loudly to be reckoned with. For example, young people in the Vietnam Era were the ones dying and the ones protesting. Much scholarship has been done on that turbulent time period due to the civil unrest. Teenagers and college students created a big stir in streets and on campuses across the country, because they had no say if they were to be drafted or not. If the young people had not depended on the older generation, the unrest may not have taken the form that it did, i.e., violent demonstrations, sit-ins, boycotts etc. Understanding the young people puts the violence in perspective, but it does so within the backdrop of the rest of the story. They complained that they were dying without representation. So, we can understand what the youth are by understanding what they are not, as well. And, as we all do, the young people grow, and they become the older generation that grapples with the issues of its youth. The cycle continues.

If one could look only at the youth and better understand any culture, the world would be a lot easier place in which to live, but it is not that easy. As the teenagers and college students begin to mature, they begin to take a more complicated framework of ideas, one that includes a more refined set of morals and an economic accountability that had never been in existence. That means that they start to look at things in a different way than they did just ten years before. They, in turn, react to teenagers and college students, many times their own children, as had their own parents reacted to them. That is to be expected. Yet, when the emerging adults remember the problems they encountered as they yelled out to be heard, they start to effectuate changes on behalf of the society's youth. That betters society as a whole. Let's face it: any society is better off without violence in the streets. In the long run, things may get better as a result. Then, we could say that the youth are an integral part of any society, and understanding the youth does lead one to understand a society in a deeper manner. But, why stop there? Those teenagers become adults, and their views change as their age does. Their class in life changes. We simply need to remember that all the classes fit together to make one big macrocosm.

When we study a famous line out of a poem or a play, the saying itself may seem so profound that it makes us just stop and think for a minute. Young people are like that. They hold a lot of vitality, and they have a huge influence on any culture in the world. But, like that line out of a poem, young people tell us more when analyzed in comparison to the whole context. We understand Tennyson's claim that "it is better to have loved and lost (that love) than to have never loved at all" if we know that the whole poem is about the death of Tennyson's best friend, one he mourned over for thirty years. Looking at the whole picture just seems to give a lot more information.

Question

Political leaders should never reveal everything to the public.

Answer:

Every society and every circumstance are always different when it comes to accountability and information. At times, national security can be compromised by a leak in information. Other times, however, the public has a right to know if something will harm the people. A society is always learning what exactly should and should not be communicated to the general population. Let's look at the security factor and then the public's right to know.

With the changing climate every day in our modern world of surveillance techniques, we are able to monitor threats that were impossible to monitor until the just the last ten years or so. Consequently, we can observe terrorist factions that would have had us scrambling for cover thirty years ago. Our equipment allows us to even eavesdrop on their conversations, always keeping tabs on their movements and their future plans. We need not worry the public with things that are in our direct line of sight, so to speak. That stands in stark contrast to the Cold War and the public's continual hanging on to information about the Soviet Union. People then felt as if they had to know, as if it was necessary to know every little detail about the enemy. Now, it simply is not the same scenario. We have the capability to predict what will happen. If the government were to tell the public every minor detail, the government would in essence be telling the enemy, as well. In sensitive cases like these, the call should be made on an individual basis, always weighing the outcome in every circumstance. By remaining silent, most often the government may be able to catch a bigger fish, perhaps even more fish with the use of a wider net. The good of all the people should preclude but not prevent the public's right to know.

Fortunately, we have a government run by the people. Our right to safety is directly linked to our right to know what affects us. Therefore, we have official intelligence agencies that track weather, crime, money, other countries, and even other government agencies. By these agencies, we can protect our crops, investments, and personal property—not to mention our person—and also track how well our representatives protect and serve us. The spirit of these agencies is rooted in our right to pursue our own interests and whatever makes us happy. These come from our daily activities like working, school, or just taking a day off. Our government has the responsibility to let us know when our daily lives could be interrupted by some catastrophic event. More aptly put, that is the line that we have drawn for ourselves where we as John or Jane Q. Public have our right to know what could affect us. One could argue that we always have a right to know everything, but we need to remember that telling the public what we know means telling the very people who we are trying to catch.

One really hates to look at numbers when talking about human life. Giving up even one life is too painful to think of. That is why the public has a right to know when any results could be catastrophic. But, too much information too soon could be just as detrimental as never saying a word. As a result, we have to look at numbers and do the best we can for everyone involved.

Question

Most people do not understand what they read if the content is out of their field. As a result, scientific ideas have little use, because they relate to such a small percentage of people.

Answer:

It is true that many different things are difficult to understand due to their esoteric content. However, the things that are difficult to understand are usually written for the people in that field. But, that does not mean that these subjects are of little use; they are simply of little use to those people who cannot understand the material. These statements need more qualification.

In the last thirty or forty years, the world has almost completely changed, especially in the scientific fields. The developments we have made have allowed us to scrutinize the world around us so exhaustively that it takes a lifetime to delve so deeply into the matters and the realms simply to keep on advancing. For instance, the discovery of the atom and then the splitting thereof has opened new fields in nuclear science. Looking at something a little closer to every day life, we see that the computer has become a science all its own, but that does not mean that the scientific principles are of no use to a person who can't understand the complicated jargon. I still use the computer to write assignments, but I do not grasp the complicated concepts that one programmer may use communicating to another programmer. The automobile is another prime example. With 250 million automobiles in America, the United States is literally a nation on the move. Drivers from 16 to 80 cruise the highways and the byways every day although only a handful understand the technical terms used in periodicals like Popular Mechanics. Does that mean the information is useless? That is a tough question. In technical lingo, the information means little to the average Joe or Jane. Broken down into understandable English, into layman's terms, the information may be invaluable. The usefulness of any information would of course depend on one's ability to ascertain what is being said. That is the beautiful thing about language. It gives people a sense of identity. For example, two physicians, namely specialists like cardiologists, could communicate more with subject specific language than by speaking in layman's terms. It is a result of cultivating the intake about the subject. The information then becomes an intimate knowledge of the field. These circles of specialists are the ones that keep that specific field improving. They discuss their craft or their science without the encumbrances of small talk. They need not talk around a subject, because they can examine it in detail—but only with each other. Other communication regarding the content is superfluous to them—and rightfully so. The ideas then may have little use if they are presented to a normal Joe in a meticulously designed package, one that is identifiable only to a certain professor or professional. The average individual is usually offended if someone tries to condescend. Does that indicate the message is useless? Maybe it is, but only in that circumstance. I need to address a couple of items in closing.

People's pride generally makes them seek out their own, for whatever reason. Doctors, lawyers, mechanics, and nutritionists all have certain fields of knowledge in common that help them define themselves. Fathers, brothers, sisters, and mothers do, too. The members identify one another due to the common ground they share. It is the crossing over from one group to the next that necessitates enlarging the vocabulary to include a bigger group. The skilled communicator is the first to admit that. Finding the common ground outside the smaller group is the challenge.

Question

States must ensure that their capital cities receive the money they need in order to thrive, because the capital city is the cradle of a state's heritage.

Answer:

Lack of money to keep up a lot of our downtown areas in major cities is a problem that affects us all. It is a bad thing to witness the decay of these areas, because they have at some time or another been areas that have culturally marked the surrounding environment as historical for some reason or another. Philadelphia is a perfect example. Without the allocation of desperately needed funds, the waste may continue.

The average individual in every state would like to be able to look at the capital city and be proud to claim it as his own. Sadly enough, many of the nation's capital cities are overrun by poverty and disrepair. What once was a thriving metropolis has a lot of barren land, perhaps populated only by empty warehouses and homeless people. They live around and walk over, sometimes even sleep on, what might have once been sacred ground or a thriving, bustling business center in times gone by. The homeless are not the only ones there. As the industry moves outward, so does the law enforcement. Crime creeps right into its place. It is not so hard to understand. The lack of funds to keep up the area has caused the law-abiding citizen to find a safe haven elsewhere. So, lawlessness takes over. Now, the problem of losing the heritage is overshadowed by other more immediate concerns like drugs, prostitution, and perhaps murder. The situation, as complex as it may be, is relatively simple to sum up: either the states need to earmark more money for the capital cities or the cities are subject to this sort of decline. The answer is not so easy. The source of this required revenue is all too vague, and most often the fixes are temporary. Further, as industry moves out of the city, the jobs go, as well. The people move outward and buy a house closer to the new work location. Some cities have begun to give tax incentives to middle class homebuyers that move into the cities, particularly in the downtown areas. In addition, new neighborhood type police stations have moved into what were once residential houses. The effort has been successful. People feel a lot safer. The poorer residents have welcomed the new middle class neighbors, because property values have increased. Not only that, but the crime has decreased. How has this had any effect on the culture of the neighborhoods? People have started to embrace these landmarks to a greater extent at an earlier stage. That is what is most significant: they do it at an earlier stage. The monetary problems are not so monumental if they are addressed in a timely manner before things are in a state of emergency. These are all positive signs of a society that has become a little more conscientious about preserving its past. Of course, this means that it will also be more vigilant to avoid those same problems in the future. It is a problem for everyone to be aware of. By preserving our collective culture, we make everyone feel included in our pluralistic society. By looking a little ahead, we have been able to avoid replaying the same situations that have caused us problems in the past. By preserving certain areas, the problems no longer appear to be only "their" problem or one only pertaining to that "other" race. They belong to all of us. We all become a part of the solution when we are all part of the culture. Sharing of the responsibility comes from sharing the culture.

Question

In the same fashion that the United Nations has been organized, the nations of the world should set up a training center to develop leaders to solve the most imminent dangers our world faces.

Answer:

In theory, a training center to develop world leaders is an excellent idea. However, the realization of it could revolve around two problems, and these are two problems the United Nations has. Basically, the conflict of political ideology could destroy any possibility of fruitful teaching at the center. Moreover, defining the role of the student upon graduation from the training center is something on which the participating countries could find it impossible to agree. Further exploration of these two problems could prove fruitful.

The UN leaders are always trained and educated prior to arriving at the UN, but any new training center would be responsible for instilling the ideology by which the graduates are expected to function in their new capacity. This is where the problem lies. The new trainees must have a common ground on which to agree. This would be extremely difficult, because the trainees would be proactive in their responses. In other words, they would be heading out to solve the world's problems rather than only to create a peaceful environment or to drive out an invader from a weaker country. If then, the trainee were there to solve a problem and not simply turn it around, how would the new trainees be taught to handle the situation? One political party might be inclined to crush any situation with brute force, the other to hold an election, and the third to crush and indoctrinate. This takes us into the classroom of a training center. The conundrum is the same. Each country comes in with a little different perspective on what is happening around the world. The communist trainee may object to handling the situation the same way that a democratic trainee would, not to forget the socialist. Nevertheless, that takes us to the teachers at the training center. What type of background should be mandatory? Let's say that a group goes to aid the starving in Somalia and it is repeatedly attacked. Do they fight back? Are they limited? These are questions that the UN faces every day, but the answer is workable with the UN mainly because they are reacting to the situation. The primal force behind a training center is to solve the problem.

The UN was built on the premise of providing peace in war-torn areas and maintaining stability in peaceful areas. When unrest escalates into violence, the countries that go in as peacekeepers already have a specified goal they want to accomplish. Their mission is defined, limited, and instituted according to a certain plan previously agreed upon by all of the participants in the peacekeeping force. This is the beauty of the UN operations. Therefore, the actions are swift and usually successful. For any new contingency of negotiators or peacekeepers going in to a situation, the role would have to be defined in the exact same way or else these countries would have recent graduates in a volatile situation and only a limited capability, if that. Would they carry guns? Then, as with the UN now, the questions would arise as to who would lead, how accountable the leaders would be, and to whom. All of these factors are certainly flashpoints in setting up such a major project. The project is not impossible but improbable. Sometimes, with too many chiefs, the people do not know whom to follow.

Trying to help people is a noble thing. We bear the responsibility of helping those who cannot help themselves. That is what our country is founded on. We do need to be sure to set very realistic goals in attempting to help others, so we do not end up coming out on the short end of the stick. Clearly defined goals and roles will head us on the right road.

Question

The way people think about things is determined more by the immediate environment around them than by their make-up.

Answer:

This is an age-old debate that has divided psychologists for years. On the one hand, environmentalists believe that a person can be "made" from his environment. On the other hand, other psychologists believe that people are predetermined to act a certain way due to the experiences they endured over the first few years of life. Both sides have valid points, but more can be said.

Without a doubt, many people are influenced by their surroundings. This is particularly obvious in teenagers and children. For example, if one were raised in a prejudiced family, s/he would probably be prejudiced, as well. The types of response people have seen others get with the same mindset precondition the way that people view and act on things. Hypothetically speaking, if an individual were looking for respect and he grew up in an area where violent people were respected, he would probably act violently. This would be conditioned in him, because he had seen that sort of behavior rewarded—at least he would call that respect a reward. Conversely, in that same neighborhood, if a young man had always been taught by his grandmother to respect older people, he could act accordingly, even after if his grandmother had passed away. If the teaching had taken root, he might be apt to keep it and act on it for the rest of his life, although that is not necessarily true. Behaviorists maintain that people like the one in the last example have already had time to internalize things around them, such as the actions and thoughts of others that will determine the way they think for the rest of their lives. Looking at both sides of the coin, however, we could observe that people do not necessarily follow one of the examples given. Let's examine a point. A person could grow up in an area all of his life until the age of 18. Then, he could move to an area that completely challenged his belief system. It is possible for him to accept the ideas of those around his new environment if he hears the same thing long enough. The environmentalists' theories do not necessarily have to cancel out the Freudians' theories. A real example may illustrate this point. Two twins met after having been separated for years. One grew up very poor and the other grew up very wealthy. The two thought almost identically about a number of things. It would appear at first sight that the outcome only supports Freud's idea that we are made in the early years of our lives. But, the next example shatters that myth. Siblings constantly grow up having the same academic and moral teachings; however, one turns out to be a productive citizen and the other a convicted felon. A common ground exists between both schools of thought, and that explains the contradictory evidence. I would like to share some final observations.

We all are products of those things and people around us. The complaining co-worker can negatively influence even the happiest and most positive person in the world. That is simply common sense. One has to consciously try to overcome these types of obstacles, but it may take a lot of effort, especially if environmentalists are correct.

Question

Much of the world's culture is being lost as more and more people move about. The world has become so mobile that people are losing their cultural identities. Governments of countries should act to preserve their cultures so that the past will not be lost forever and tomorrow's youth will have a sense of identity.

Answer:

It is paramount that a person have a sense of cultural identity. Tragically, we lose history each and every day. Many times, our history is lost forever in that languages become extinct, historical sites are forgotten, and a significant story is never told. Luckily enough, with a little foresight, some organizations like UNESCO and local historical societies have begun efforts to record languages, preserve sites, and avoid any other losses that may be preventable in the same areas. Interestingly enough, though, is the question of where do we draw the line in spending our limited resources to preserve our heritage.

Man has had the tendency to record as long as written history has actually existed. We see this through crude scratching on cave walls that have existed presumably from the beginning of man's existence. Humanity has had the good fortune to learn from these types of recordings. In fact, some people spend all of their lives searching the past, putting it into perspective, reconstructing events that have shaped the world today as we know it. Without the dedication of the historians who have studied people like Hitler, other societies may have been destined to repeat the same sort of atrocities. So, looking at the concept of recorded history as being somewhat of a reference tool, one could obviously see that humanity is better off on many different levels. Not only does man have the knowledge to avoid another holocaust but also the knowledge to succeed using the same formulae as others before who have succeeded. For instance, if no one had recorded Albert Einstein's work, perhaps the world may have had to wait centuries again for his sort of genius to come along. Similarly, the accomplishments of a particularly disadvantaged individual may inspire posterity of the same race. Martin Luther King Jr. stands out as a person of color who stood up and changed life for African Americans forever. People like this and their heroic deeds should definitely be told and retold. Further, places where these people have made a stand against injustice remind us that freedom is not cheap. Countless people whose names have long been forgotten by the public died there for a noble cause. Places like The Alamo and Valley Forge bring to mind the struggles endured and overcome at those very spots. They are visual reminders of the enduring human spirit. These same problems that were defeated at these places still exist all around the world. Though innumerable battles have been fought along the way, even wars, the fight still continues. In places like the former Yugoslavia, ethnic cleansing created situations reminiscent of Hitler's and Marx's campaigns. People around the world remembered WWII and acted against these terrible murderers. Still, we fight the same problems again and again. Resources to fight these wars against tyranny and oppression are most often scant. Then, one has to wonder: record culture or fight tyranny?

With only so much capital, governments frequently find themselves debating over preserving culture or spending the money elsewhere. It is the age-old question: Does the kid get shoes or does the family get food? The answer is usually in the questions in situations like this. The answer is simple: The governments should take care of the most expedient problems first. In super power countries like America, funds are usually allocated for cultural preservation. I could not be any happier to say that grants are available for artists. Museums are funded. Major universities have the wherewithal to send graduate students to places around the world to record near extinct languages. In contrast, developing countries struggle to keep law and order. For many of them, adequate healthcare is a luxury, at least for the general populace. Likewise, some of these countries are continually fighting insurrection. To be blunt, they probably do not have the resources to pour into cultural projects. Consequently, countries that do have the resources need to help if possible.

People should not lose sight of the important things to lay hold of those ideals. An ideal is just that:

ideal. Ideal here defines the best of all possibilities. If preservation is not possible because people need the money to eat, it is just not possible. Undoubtedly, countries like America, France, and England will send scientists and scholars to help record and preserve, but ultimately the responsibility is all of ours, because we are one giant people.

Question

The strength of a country comes from its response to the wide range of people's actions.

Answer:

A country's strength emanates from so many different factors that they are practically immeasurable. For this reason, in order to respond to the statement, I need to first define the word "strength." One could look at the traditional idea of strength and talk about military might, but that would limit the range of topics. Like a person, a country need not be mighty to be strong. Some of history's strongest leaders were physically weak, perhaps overweight or even sickly. Let's define strength as stability. To do so, we need to take into account some the factors that mark a country as stable.

The indicators economists employ to define the stability of a country are stability in trade, monetary exchange rate, and political soundness. These same factors should also be implemented to react to the comment above. All of these factors indeed coalesce to make a nation function as one unit. Without the unity of the nation's citizens, a country could disintegrate into a fragmented society where in the individual ingredients are fighting against each other to get ahead in contrast to working together. A unified society will consist of assorted constituents, but they will be working together to accomplish certain goals that are profitable for everyone. Trade is a perfect example. The give and take involved in trade should work toward the benefit of both parties. But, in the event an extreme third party would rather rob and pillage, the other parties' strength comes through their unity in opposing the third party. Therefore, the stability or strength through trade can continue. Taking the same trade element into account, one could assume a third party chooses not to trade or even socialize at all, but rather stay secluded. The other two parties would benefit the most by allowing this sort of radical behavior to go unchallenged, as long as it is peaceful. Money exchange is not something taken lightly either.

Just like the trade within the country is an economic indicator, the trade outside of the country acts as a valve to control the pressure brought on by monopolies. Generally speaking, the trade inside of a country mirrors the trade outside of a country. This forces people who deal with one another to deal fairly, because more business looms at the border, so to speak. Therefore, any groups that hold an unfair trade advantage within the country know to act honestly due to the competition from outside parties. This in turn affects a free trade and keeps the currency stable. The exchange rate vicariously remains pretty well the same, and outside interests are drawn into the trade equation, thereby adding to the ingredients for success. All of this takes us into political stability.

Some people always get involved, and others always go along. Those, however, that choose to react to politics in a violent manner are the same ones that can create tumult in any country. A country's swift reaction to suppress unacceptably violent reformist techniques lends to its strength as a stable entity. The most common factor in stability is peaceful reform. Everyone gets a chance at the pie. They all agree to gracefully bow out if the majority wins. Dealing with any other action needs to be united effort. When it is, it is successful.

The old common definition of strength is not a sound one in defining the strength of a nation. The enduring aspects of a country are those rooted in cooperation, peaceful reform, and continued trade in and out of the country. With these elements, countries are destined for stability.

Question

Most everyone wants to work hard to attain the good life. Most people do not know, however, that the good life really makes people weak in the long run.

Answer:

The good life as most people see it includes the luxuries that make life a little easier or the ride a little smoother, but to others the good life can mean this and so much more. The luxuries that help us in our daily routine could lead one to be a little lazy. Nevertheless, these same luxuries could open up a lot of free time for those individuals who want to use their time more creatively. Closer detail should shed a lot more light on the subject.

The idea of a luxury is usually something that makes life a little easier, but something that one could really do without. Electric can openers, gas propelled blowers, and a hundred other similar products could be considered somewhat excessive in referring to what one normally uses as a tool, and, if a guy always took the easy way out like blowing off the driveway rather that sweeping it and getting a little exercise, he could get lazy. A lot of people spend money on gadgets to help them out, things like electric choppers and food processors. Using those types of things is not wrong. In fact, the professional cook probably thanks heaven twenty times a day for the added help in the kitchen. To be sure, the sixty year old with a snow blower saves himself a lot of time and a lot of energy. And, I am not quite certain that his use of it will make him weak. It is possible that a lot of people who work hard jobs want conveniences like these to make a life a lot easier, especially after doing physical labor for forty years. In such an example, they are reaping the fruits of their hard work. If a young man around the age of sixteen uses all electric appliances every, single day, he might be a little weaker than the average kid. At that young age, he needs a little hard work to get his blood flowing. That is assuming, however, that he does no other exercise. Working on assumptions is not a good idea. In short, conveniences and luxuries, whatever term one might apply, do not necessarily make people lazy, nor do they always hurt people. They could. We need to analyze another class of individuals.

Living the so-called good life could mean that a person has to work a lot, long and hard hours. In cases like that, the conveniences do make life a lot easier for one specific reason: the person has more important things to do. A high profile lawyer may have months at a stretch that he is home for maybe five hours per night. One would be so bold as to venture to say that his electric dishwasher would not hurt him. It frees his time. A professional body-builder may spend five hour per day in the gym working out, pushing and pulling his way to success. He might buy a food processor to free up his time, especially if he eats five or six meals daily. All in all, our lifestyles are too diverse to say that the good life could make us weak.

The good life, as many people see it, is having utensils that help us or make us more comfortable. If these luxuries help us achieve our goals by expanding our free time so that we can do what we want, I think almost everyone would want to live a luxurious lifestyle. But, then again, the American dream is a very personal one.

Question

In order to prevent oppression by any government, everybody in a society has a right to exercise civil disobedience against unfair statutes.

Answer:

In a society that is formed by the people, we walk a line of blurred distinction where what may seem oppressive to one individual may seem libertine to another. Thus, every citizen needs to walk with extreme care as to how s/he handles a seemingly unfair regulation. In accordance with any dangers that might result from our actions, we need to first inspect the definition of civil disobedience. Then, we can observe the result of civil disobedience and make a judgment from there as to whether or not we do indeed have the right to exercise disobedience.

Civil disobedience, as Henry David Thoreau defines it, is an action whereby a citizen refuses to comply with a law. Martin Luther King Jr.'s refusal to stop his marches, because he did not have a permit was civil disobedience. The refusal of many African Americans to sit at the back of the bus was civil disobedience. These people disobeyed a civil ordinance that they felt demeaned them as citizens. They acted on a collective conscience that determined the laws were unfair, because the laws targeted a specific minority group. Consequently, the minority group suffered unfairly. These actions on the part of African Americans were successful. The protests were organized, peaceful, and designed to affect a change through civil action—not criminal. This is an important distinction. Now that we have established the general framework for the idea of civil disobedience, we need to examine the context that one could apply civil disobedience. The African Americans were moving toward the status of equality in America. Mahatma Gandhi exercised civil disobedience in his campaign for India's freedom from England.

The campaign was much like the African American movement. The Indians did not have many of the freedoms that the colonists did. The move was to elevate the indigenous population to the status of equality with another population. The wording of the statement says everyone has a right to exercise civil disobedience against unfair statutes. In the United States, it is not that simple. We have a fair society, one in which all people are treated equally under the law. This is not to say that situations do not exist where people endure discrimination. They do have legal recourse if that happens. To be blunt, most people could take the stance that they will not do something, follow the speed limit, for example, because the law oppresses them in some way. Too many may take this type of logic as a license to actually break the law. One need only look at the link between one feeling that he has the right to be civilly disobedient and the long-term result of that disobedience.

We can see by looking at the number of cases that overrun our courts that we are an extremely litigious society. People know they have recourse if they are treated unfairly. But, if they actually felt that they could simply disregard the law because it seemed unjust, chaos would be on every street corner. We would have open violence in the street, fist fighting, stealing, speeding, drug dealing, and everything else that people could rationalize. Many people behind bars never learn their lesson about constructive living, because they think they have a right to live outside of the law. Many drug dealers say they have a right to deal drugs, because they cannot find jobs, or no one would give them jobs. We certainly do not need to fuel that fire. That sort of thinking does call for a couple closing comments though.

Over the last 200 years, we have honed our legal system, and it is now the very best in the world. It would be foolish to claim that things do not happen that sometimes shake our faith, but we cannot add superficial or emotional reasoning to support the actions that would tear down what we have worked so hard to build up. We have recourse: the system. People do listen. Plus, if a situation is bad enough, enough people will get involved to make changes faster. We just need to follow the plan that our founding fathers set for us.

Question

If there is never opposition to an argument, the worth of that argument is never fully appreciated.

Answer:

The intrinsic value of something usually speaks for itself, but it may be heard a lot more clearer if it endures trial by fire. Flight, medicine, and nuclear science are three areas that certainly bear record to this premise. But, to say that humanity could not appreciate flight, medicine, and nuclear science as much if no opposition had existed seems to be a blanket statement that might not withstand scrutiny, even though it contains some truth.

Some people thrive on opposition, and, without it, they would never push themselves as far as they could. These are individuals that appreciate the value of innovation. They push through to new horizons, constantly expanding their limits, and they seek to prove scoffers wrong. These are people like Thomas Edison, Henry Ford, and Ted Turner. They are pioneers, groundbreakers, who forge new paths. If we were to trail them for a day, we might hear them eject negative people from their midst. Actions

like that are common with uncommon success stories, because these pacesetters know that something
can be done. They have proven it time and time
again. It is no wonder that they would not tolerate
fear, doubt, unbelief, and complaining by their sub-
ordinates. These warriors are spurred to achieve
when colleagues express doubt or scorn. Yet, that
does not explain whether or not the conquerors
appreciate their ideas more than if they had no opposition. Obviously, they appreciate the challenge.
Competition forces them to achieve more success
faster. Another group of individuals exists who probably do not have any feeling one way or another.

The individuals who know that progress has
been made in a certain area but don't care about its
history will probably not appreciate some things
any more or less than they do now. Most folks know
that sailors of the time scoffed at Christopher
Columbus, because the general consensus was that
the earth was flat. Nowadays, most people do not
care at all if there was opposition to Columbus' theory. For this generation, our present ideas are so
embedded that appreciation is just out the window.
There is a point where the appreciation for an idea

or a concept is no longer applicable to the whole scenario, and people take things for granted. Moreover, even the innovators are constantly looking ahead, so they might even lose interest after a while. We can appreciate the value of Madame Curie's ideas and the ordeal she went through to make her findings. We are thankful that she had the tenacity to plunge into her work, regardless of the trials she went through, especially to the point of terminal illness. But, the brightness of that innovation fades, at least for a little while. It can resurface, however, when we see how healthy our youngsters are. The appreciation for the Wright Brothers should flare up after a twenty-hour plane trip. Yet, one may find it hard to appreciate the fact that there was any opposition that slowed down the progress. These are isolated in our minds for a while, but only until we search out why we have life so easy. Then, we can appreciate the ideas.

Any innovator who has brought forth a new invention or a new concept that has changed the course of history probably endured a lot of opposition. I am more inclined to say that we appreciate an idea, because the inventor withstood the opposition. His self-confidence was usually the deciding factor in the success of his idea.

Parting Thoughts

When you read the writing prompt, formulate a pattern of development. Stick with your plan. You will succeed. Good luck.

Tim Avants
avants2002@yahoo.com

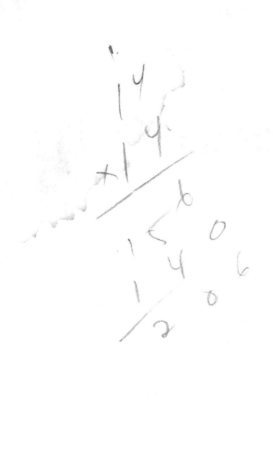

7 × 9

2
15
× 15
76
5 0
2 2 5

2
15
× 15
7 5
1 5 0
2 2 5

4
15 9
9
1